AF785123

# CONTENTS





Second Edition, 1983.

An Organization of Americans for Legal Reform

Primary Author: Mathew Valencic
Editor: Paul Hasse

*Special thanks to the following for their invaluable comments and advice:*

Niles W. Bond, Ray Chamberlin, Sandra DeMent, Natalie Genner, Fred Grabowski, Beth Lerch, Maria Merkowitz, Lawrence M. Noble, Joseph P. Saba, Douglas M. Steenland, Joan Crosby Tibbetts and Robert S. Tigner.

Cover: Carla Badaracco

Sixth Printing, 1983.

ISBN 0-910073—00-7

# Introduction

The purpose of this booklet is to provide tips to people seeking legal counsel. It is full of questions that you should ask yourself before hiring a lawyer. It is full of questions to ask lawyers before hiring one. If you obtain a clear understanding *and* a written description of what the lawyer is to do in your case, you can avoid many conflicts that frequently arise. Knowledge of the most common difficulties besetting consumers of legal services will put you in a better position to protect your own interests.

HALT's program of reform advocates simplifying American legal procedures and making the legal system more accessible and responsive to American citizens. Lawyers often complicate matters unnecessarily and make the cost of obtaining justice prohibitive, while the "adversary"ethic of lawyers frequently does more to obscure than to clarify the truth. These obstacles to justice have provoked American's increasing bitterness towards the legal system and lawyers.

While HALT presses for reforms which enable people to handle more of their own legal affairs, we realize that certain circumstances make some form of legal counsel necessary or desirable. This booklet will help you consider alternatives to hiring a lawyer. But its principal aim is to help you select a fully qualified lawyer and, above all, prepare you to deal with lawyers so that you can maintain full control of your legal affairs.

Remember, there is nothing awesome or mysterious about lawyers. They may wear funny suits, or speak in language that you don't understand. But so do auto mechanics and used car dealers. Lawyers can be expected to give complicated answers to simple questions. Insist upon clarity. Make sure you fully understand everything being discussed.

Lawyers sell legal services, just as mechanics offer services to fix your car or make sure that it runs smoothly. You choose the one you want. You are the boss. It is your money, your property, your rights—even your life or livelihood—that may be at stake. You have to check things out thoroughly. *You* have to keep an eye on them to make sure the service you get is dependable and worth what it costs.

# I. DO YOU NEED A LAWYER?

You can, with some effort and diligence, handle many legal matters yourself. At most, you may need the advice of an experienced friend or the information in procedural instruction booklets. Or you may consider simply consulting a lawyer, at reduced time and expense, while you actually work out your own legal affairs.

***Can you do it yourself?***

Increasingly, routine legal matters can be conducted without the services of a lawyer. Simple wills and contracts, incorporations and bankruptcies, uncontested divorces, probate, minor disputes, immigration, and many other common matters can be completed quickly and inexpensively. Filling-in the blanks on standard forms and filing them properly is often all that's required.

Minor disputes can often be resolved in small claims courts without lawyers. In various states, these courts operate under different names, such as county court, municipal court, justice of the peace or magistrate's court. The jurisdiction of small claims courts is limited to minor amounts of money or property. The amount varies from state to state, ranging form $500 to $5000.

***Arbitration may resolve a dispute.***

Counselling, mediation, and arbitration also can be used to resolve disputes, large and small, without the prolonged and expensive battles of lawyers in court. Groups like the American Arbitration Association have settled controversial disputes over business contracts, and have now expanded their arbitration program to include consumer and housing disputes. Both arbitration and mediation are being used more frequently to resolve many different kinds of disputes outside the courts.

Too often, in the heat of dispute, lawyers are obtained as "hired guns" who pursue the resolution of legal matters motivated by financial gain rather than by concern for justice. This course of action proves more frustrating, more embittering, and more expensive than the original grievance. Remember that many disputes can be resolved through established legal procedures without lawyers. Revenge and hired guns are best left to movie westerns.

***Choose a lawyer for the right reasons.***

A competent and ethical lawyer *can* play a valuable role in more complicated legal affairs, particularly if you are confronted with litigation conducted by an opposing party's lawyer. For simpler civil matters, you may hire a lawyer because you do not have the time, or the inclination, to handle those matters yourself. But always consider the alternatives to hiring a lawyer. A "complex" matter may be easier and less costly to resolve than it would first appear, or than a lawyer would have you believe. Disputes may be resolved without litigation and simple civil procedures can be completed in a "do-it-yourself" manner.

Whether you need a lawyer, or exactly when you should seek one's advice, depends upon your particular situation. In general, a lawyer's services are unnecessary for any civil matter that does not involve considerable money or property. In many cases where substantial sums of money are involved, some individuals can still competently handle their own legal business. However, when in doubt or when lacking adequate time, it is probably best to seek legal help of some kind before matters become complicated by delay or misguided action. This is especially true in situations which involve, for example, a jury trial or a counter-suit. A wrong initial move could waive your rights in the matter entirely.

## II. SHOPPING AROUND

Once you have determined that you want the services of a lawyer, the "shopping" process should begin immediately. The veil of mystery that has shrouded the law and lawyers must be lifted by you. In the past, this veil has been used to obscure an important fact: that legal services, especially the ones that most people require, should operate in a buyer's market.

The ability, training, and integrity of individual lawyers vary greatly. Chief Justice Warren Burger once estimated that more than one-half of America's trial lawyers are incompetent. Thus picking one from the Yellow Pages is a bit like playing Russian roulette with your legal rights.

***'Shop' for a lawyer carefully.***

If you want to *choose* a lawyer rather than take potluck, you have to do some serious shopping. 'Serious shopping' requires that you rigorously follow a certain sequence. (1) Determine what type of legal assistance you are looking for. (2) Gather together a list of likely candidates from various sources. (3) Prepare questions and interview each candidate. (4) Compare their answers, their personal and professional qualities and their fees. (5) Choose the one you think you can trust to competently perform the service you need at the lowest cost.

There are several ways to conduct your shopping for legal services. Here are a few suggestions to help you locate the names of lawyers or find substitute services that may do just as well:

***1.*** *Talk to a friend or neighbor* who has been through legal matters or hired a lawyer before. Ideally, you should find someone who has been in a situation similar to yours. The vast majority of the average citizen's needs fall into a few categories that confront almost everyone (e.g., wills, probate, divorce, real estate, minor disputes, etc.). It should not be too difficult to locate someone with relevant experience and advice to offer. If you do not know such a person, you can find the names and addresses of people who have had cases similar to yours by checking the dockets at the court clerk's office.

***Ask friends who've had similar legal problems.***

You can learn many things from experienced consumers of legal services. They can tell you what they have been through, and what you can expect. They may refer you to the lawyer who handled their legal matter, or suggest cheaper and easier alternatives that they have discovered. They can advise you about questions to ask and practices to guard against. But make sure that these people give you an honest and critical assessment. Someone simply pleased with a victorious "hired gun" may steer you into a costly, and ugly, affair.

**2.** *Speak with "non-lawyer" professionals.* A business person, counselor, doctor, or minister is likely to have had some experience with legal matters, or to know people who have been in situations similar to yours. For example, on family matters (divorce, adoption, etc.), a minister, marriage counselor, or social worker may be able to provide valuable advice or make recommendations and referrals. Similarly, business people that you know, or an officer at the local bank, may be able to offer advice or referrals on financial matters.

***Ask businessmen, professionals, or social workers.***

Referrals to lawyers from other professionals is a common and helpful practice. However, a strong word of warning is necessary. Many professionals have business relationships with lawyers that rate higher on their list of priorities than straightforward advice to you. In many instances, this does not pose any difficulties. But sometimes it results in fees, "kickbacks," or free services from the lawyer to the person who referred you. Of course, you end up paying for this indirectly.

Also, lawyers will often refer you to other lawyers. A "referral fee" or kickback may be paid by the second lawyer to the first for forwarding business in this manner. The extra charge can be figured easily and quietly into your bill. This practice is strictly unacceptable, but that doesn't prevent it from happening. It should be reported to the local bar association whenever it is discovered.

However, a lawyer that has been *working* on your case may ethically accept a "referral fee" for the time involved in obtaining another lawyer for you and transferring the case. The lawyers' code of ethics requires that you be informed about this fee *before* the transfer is made.

Professionals can be valuable sources of information, but watch for informal deals between them and the lawyers they recommend. *Always be skeptical of an arrangement in which a lawyer is recommended or required for a legal matter by someone involved in that very matter.* This is often the case, for instance, in securing a title to property and in obtaining a mortgage.

***Beware of conflicting business interests.***

Such practices prevent real competitión from working in the legal services market, thus keeping prices artificially high. Various forms of legal monopoly are being challenged in several states. You should be aware of them, and challenge them, too, if the opportunity arises. Remember, you want a recommendation in *your* best interest, not in the interest of someone else. You also want to see a legal services market that operates in a reasonable price range.

**3.** *Call local organizations* which can provide information about legal services. Citizens' groups often form to provide information about particular areas of the law (e.g., on divorce and custody matters, juvenile problems, consumer issues). These groups may hold clinics or offer referral services. Some groups are experimenting with citizen dispute resolution centers. At these centers, members of a community work with mediators trained to help people resolve private disputes.

Many public interest organizations and public interest law firms provide legal services, often in specialized areas. Some can refer you to the most experienced and qualified lawyers in a particular field, if your case is more than routine. If your case is especially significant, an organization like the American Civil Liberties Union (ACLU) or the National Association for the Advancement of Colored People (NAACP) may give you free representation. These organizations are also excellent sources of general information.

***Ask citizens' groups for assistance or referral.***

For routine matters, you can approach the local offices of consumer agencies or participants in community action programs. If they cannot provide you with the information or the help that you need, they can at least direct you to someone likely to be of assistance.

**4.** *Contact local, state, and federal government agencies.* Most government agencies maintain offices that handle routine inquiries. They can direct you to local sources of help.

Certain government offices are established to deal specifically with legal matters for citizens. Neighborhood Justice Centers, for example, are federally funded experiments in settling disputes without representation by private lawyers. Legal Aid helps to provide legal services for low-income citizens. And programs funded by the national Legal Services Corporation are being developed around the country to expand and improve Legal Aid services.

***Are you eligible for public legal assistance?***

To find out about public legal assistance, call local organizations, the county or municipal courthouse, or the District (or County) Attorney's office. The eligibility guidelines for public assistance depend upon where you live and upon the size of your family and earnings. But even if you do not qualify for free or at-cost legal service, these offices should be able to provide dependable information and probably referrals.

Another source of information about particular lawyers can be found at the local courthouse. Most of the employees at a courthouse are familiar with the local lawyers. They have seen them in action time and again, and can tell you which ones are competent. Tips from judges, marshalls, court clerks, court stenographers, bailiffs, etc., can all be valuable, especially if you need a trial lawyer. These people know which lawyers have shown real ability in the courtroom.

***Ask for referrals at the courthouse.***

**5.** *Try a local lawyer referral service.* Most local bar associations offer a referral service which can be of some initial help. These services are usually listed at the beginning of the "Lawyers" section in the Yellow Pages. You can also find out about referral services through the local bar association.

A word of warning is necessary here. Bar association referral services simply provide lists of the names and phone numbers of lawyers. Only minimal qualifications are required to be listed. No real evaluation of the lawyer's competence or honesty is made. If the local bar has a Citizen's Advisory Committee, run by "non-lawyers," you ought to contact them.

The *Martindale-Hubbell Law Directory* is a well-known listing of lawyers, a sort of "Who's Who" of the legal fraternity. Frankly, it is of little direct help since the 'rating' system (a, b, or c) is applied only to those few lawyers who wish to be rated. Moreover, a lawyer's rating is based on the recommendations of his fellow lawyers, and not of his clients. Like a high school yearbook, the biographical information is simply provided by the attorneys themselves, but it may include the names of clients who can be contacted for referral information.

Whatever the source of referrals, it's clearly up to you to check things out. Bar association referral services, with a few exceptions, do not offer sufficient screening and selectivity to be very helpful. They should be consulted only as one step, in the initial stages, of your shopping for a lawyer.

**6.** *Call the law schools* near home or work. These can be an excellent source of information about legal services available in your community. Also, many law schools conduct legal clinical programs. These programs are designed to give law students practical courtroom experience. Under the supervision of an experienced lawyer, the students usually handle cases for "indigent" (i.e., low or no-income) persons, who would not otherwise obtain legal help. However, not *all* of these programs require that clients have a low income. It's quite possible that a law student in a university clinic may be able to handle your legal matters competently.

***A university legal clinic may be able to help.***

If you cannot obtain assistance from a clinical program, ask for the names of faculty members who teach courses in the area of law that concerns you. The professors might be able to make recommendations or referrals.

**7.** *Ask at work* about a lawyer. Many companies keep a lawyer on salary or on "retainer." Try to speak with this lawyer about your legal matter. As a fellow employee, you are more likely to get good advice and referrals from the company lawyer than from one with whom you have no connection.

***Ask your company's lawyer.***

Some companies and unions now offer "prepaid group legal plans." These are modeled on health insurance plans, where groups of people pay small regular installments into a general fund. The "legal insurance" made available through such a fund covers the costs of several legal services for participants in the plan.

Prepaid legal plans are a fairly new development. Many have very narrow or limited coverage. Read the policies carefully before you consider joining one. Note, for instance, that most plans do not cover pre-existing legal problems. Also, consider whether you can obtain the services covered as easily and inexpensively on your own if the occasion demands. Some plans cover things you should be able to accomplish without a lawyer at all.

***Check advertisements to compare prices.***

**8.** *Have a look at advertisements in newspapers.* This can be a good method of locating routine legal services. Simple wills, incorporations, bankruptcies, uncontested divorces, probate, adoptions, etc., are services commonly advertised for a fixed fee. If your legal matter is routine, competent service can be located in this manner.

Cut-rate prices—in some instances—can mean cut-rate quality of work as well. Some offices offer low-cost legal assistance on principle, others to cut corners for additional profit. The latter may allow quantity to take precedence over quality. But many basic legal services are so simple that it is difficult to go wrong. There is no need to pay high professional fees for what is often simple clerical work.

Advertisements are just another means of *locating* lawyers and comparing their services and costs. Through them, you can get an idea of how inexpensive routine legal services can be, and you can measure this information against price quotes obtained from other lawyers and other sources. But *you* must make the final judgment about which lawyer's services can best meet your needs at an affordable price.

***'Storefront' clinics offer routine services for less.***

**9.** *Check the new 'storefront legal clinics.'* These "legal stores" will be located soon at shopping centers around the country. Most advertise routine legal services at prices well below those charged by individual lawyers. The stores concentrate on processing large volumes of routine matters (i.e., the civil affairs of most citizens). The volume allows them to cut prices. If your matter requires more than standard service, however, it will probably cost you more than the advertised fee.

Some of these clinics offer free or low-priced "one-time only" calls to their lawyers. You get a single phone conversation with a lawyer, during which you may discuss your situation and seek legal advice. From this initial call, you can determine whether your legal matter simply requires routine processing or further individual attention from a lawyer. Processing and referrals are available at the clinic.

***10.*** *Write to HALT.* HALT operates a small legal assistance referral network to help people who are having difficulty finding competent legal services. We cannot guarantee that HALT will be able to find legal assistance for you, but we can be of some help in many cases.

***Check with HALT.***

If you have tried all of the methods of locating legal assistance listed above and still feel that you need HALT's assistance, you must first send us a *short* written summary of your problem *(no more than two pages, please).* Include in your summary: (1) a description of the nature and basic circumstances of your problem; (2) the names and addresses of any attorneys that are now (or were) involved in the matter; (3) an explanation of any legal proceedings that have taken place or that are scheduled; and (4), all other important facts and dates that are relevant to the case. *Do not send any original documents or any other materials that you may want returned.*

Once HALT's staff reviews your summary, we will try to locate appropriate sources of help. If an attorney's assistance appears necessary, we will send you the name, address, and phone number of any lawyer(s) on our referral list in your area. *It will be your responsibility to contact the referrals we make to you, and to determine if a particular referral is appropriate for your situation.* And the exact business arrangements that will govern the costs and management of your legal matter are entirely for you and the lawyer you select to determine.

HALT may not always be able to locate legal assistance for all matters in all areas of the country. And when we do locate assistance, we cannot *guarantee* you a satisfactory relationship with a particular lawyer. All that HALT can do is attempt to add to your "shopping list" and urge you to use the "shopping tips" in this manual. Given your patience and cooperation, HALT will do its best to assist you. But the responsibility for decisions, and for managing your legal affairs and your attorney, rests finally with you.

When you select a lawyer, you will want to establish a special confidential relationship in which you can discuss your private legal affairs. However, if you believe that you could use moral support during the interviewing phase, you might consider asking a friend or relative to attend lawyer interviews with you. A companion may remember things you forget, or think of things that haven't crossed your mind. Also, you will have a witness to whatever the lawyer promises you, and someone to help you assess the lawyer after the interview.

# III. GETTING ORGANIZED

Once you have determined that you do want the services of a lawyer, and have tracked down several suitable candidates, you will have to narrow your options. The first step is to call the lawyers on your list for general information. You must make sure that your situation actually requires a lawyer's expertise. You will also want information from different lawyers in order to compare the

***Telephone to compare prices and services offered.***

services they offer and the prices they charge. Do these lawyers offer the services you require? What do they charge for them? Can you get a reasonable estimate of what it might cost you?

After gathering and comparing this basic information, the next step is to set up a couple of appointments with lawyers. The purpose of an appointment is for *you* to interview the lawyer. Use this opportunity to determine which lawyer you want to hire.

***Arrange a "get-acquainted" meeting.***

Many lawyers will agree to a 'get-acquainted' meeting free of charge. Others require a basic fee even for the first meeting. In either case, make the purpose of your visit clear over the phone. Ask if there will be a fee for the meeting. If there is, ask what the charge will be.

There are a number of things to keep in mind for the interviews. Questions, costs, details, possible difficulties, etc.—each of these is an important consideration. But above all, there are certain things that you should *always* remember:

***1.*** *You are doing the hiring.* You will be the boss. The lawyer will work for you, not the other way around.

***Remember: you're the boss.***

Many people are intimidated by the law and by lawyers. Many lawyers know how to take great advantage of this. Remember that *you* are doing the shopping. It is your situation that requires servicing by a sort of legal mechanic—the lawyer. There is nothing more mysterious about it than that. If you do not like the lawyer or the terms, then do not hire that lawyer.

***2.*** *Keep your records organized.* Start a file for all documents, letters, bills, etc., that are relevant to your legal problem. You might also want to file notes of important conversations and events, including dates and places. Try to keep everything in chronological order. If you keep your file organized and up-to-date, you will be able to find important papers when you need them. You'll also be able to follow the progress of your case more easily.

***Keep your original documents organized in a file.***

Unless you absolutely must, *never* leave originals of these important documents in anyone else's hands. It's better to make as many copies as are needed and refuse to permit important evidence to be taken from your possession. If you must give up an original, make a copy for your files and make a note of who has the original, why it was demanded, and when it was presented. These precautions are necessary because *you* are ultimately responsible for all original documents. You do not want original documents in the hands of a lawyer that you may decide not to hire because there may be difficulty retrieving them. The same is true of a lawyer that you do hire. In the event of a dispute with the lawyer or if you decide to change lawyers at a later point, you will need complete access to your original documents.

*3. Prepare an outline or summary of your situation.* Before you interview a lawyer, you should think through the events that led to your problem, and think about your concerns and your present circumstances. Write a brief summary of your problem that includes all important names, facts, dates, and events in chronological order. Before the interview, ask the lawyer over the telephone if there are any particular documents or records that you should bring. You should also make a list of questions that you want to ask the lawyer and take the list with you to the interview. A list of ten basic questions is given in the next section of this manual.

***Write a summary of the facts.***

If you clarify your situation in your own mind and put it on paper, you will be more likely to find the right lawyer — and you will probably save time and money. A lawyer who has been presented with a clear summary of your case should be better able to grasp the issues quickly, tell you what can be done, and suggest how to resolve the problem. Always remember that a lawyer's *time* is expensive. The better *you* organize the facts of your situation, the less time the lawyer will have to spend sorting things out. Your fee will be reduced accordingly. Also, you will be in a better position to understand what a lawyer can and will do for you, and why.

# IV. INTERVIEWING LAWYERS

One reason for going to a private lawyer is to get detailed, individual handling of legal affairs. Many people will pay more for this "extra" treatment rather than go to a legal clinic that depends upon processing large volumes of routine legal matters.

However, clerical work is clerical work. If you choose to pay $75 an hour for it instead of $10, that's up to you. But it's worth considering twice whether the higher price really gets you anything "extra."

If individual treatment is what you want, and if you are willing to pay for it, be sure that you get it. Do not allow your questions and legal affairs to be classified under easy categorizations. Demand custom-made solutions to your legal problems.

***Demand individual attention.***

Emphasize the importance and the interest that your legal affairs hold for you. Assert that you want to participate in securing or resolving them. If you ask a question, get a straight-forward answer that addresses what you have in mind. If you get pigeonholed, as often happens, you might as well have gone to a clinic. You would have received comparable service at a substantially lower cost.

Conducting an interview with your prospective lawyer is a very important task. Costs and compatibility are important factors to determine. Especially important is how cooperative the lawyer will be with involving you in the conduct of *your* legal affairs.

When you select a lawyer, you will want to establish a special confidential relationship in which you can discuss your private legal affairs. However, if you believe that you could use moral support during the interviewing phase you might consider asking a friend or relative to attend lawyer interviews with you. A companion may remember things you forget, or think of things that haven't crossed your mind. Also, you will have a witness to whatever the lawyer promises you, and someone to help you assess the lawyer after the interview.

***Take written questions.***

At the interview, you will want to ask many questions concerning your specific legal situation. Think about these questions beforehand. Write them down. Take written questions into the meeting. Time will be limited, and may be quite costly. You don't want to forget anything important. And you don't want to keep the meter running unnecessarily while you stare blankly at the lawyer's carpet trying to think of a forgotten question.

Questions regarding your specific case are very important. These should arise in the course of discussion with the lawyer. But there are several general questions to ask a prospective lawyer before delving into specifics about the legal matter in hand. There are some things you want to know about the lawyer, and about the lawyer's mode of conducting business, *before* you lay your legal affairs—and your money—on the table.

Here are a few of the most basic questions to ask:

***Is the lawyer experienced with similar cases?***

***1.*** *"Do you handle cases or matters like mine?"* This should have been asked over the phone. But it won't hurt to bring it up again. One reason is simply to assert that *you* are doing the interviewing.

Also, the lawyer may have handled a case similar to yours recently. You can ask about its outcome. How long did it take? What were the fees? What other costs accumulated? Were there any unusual difficulties involved?

This question is not intended to corner a "specialist" for you. Most people do not need a "specialist" for many civil matters. A competent attorney in general practice can handle most civil matters adequately, and the fee will be significantly lower than that of a specialist. Even lawyers who do not "specialize" may have considerable knowledge or experience in the area of law that concerns you. Some specialists however, may be able to complete a task for less expense, although charging a higher rate. Their expertise in complicated matters should enable them to do the work in a shorter period of time than a generalist.

**2.** *"Will you actually do the work?"* Determine what proportion of the work the lawyer actually will do. Be skeptical of any unwillingness to discuss details. Avoid high lawyer's fees for work done by non-professionals in the lawyer's office.

***Who will work on the case?***

At a law firm with partners and staff, insist upon interviewing the lawyer that will work on your affairs. It is a common practice in both small and large firms to have more experienced lawyers interview potential clients. The estimated fee presented is then based on the higher hourly rate of the experienced lawyer, while the actual work may be done by a young, inexperienced associate or even a paralegal. You may get competent service in a situation like this, but you will *not* be getting what you are made to believe you are paying for. Do not settle for such "front" figures. If staff members will do most of the work, insist upon meeting them, too. Even in a sole practitioner's office, it can be worth your while to talk to the secretary.

Much standard legal work is performed by secretaries and paralegals. As mentioned earlier, considerable "legal" work is simply a matter of completing and filing ready-made forms. Residential title searches, for example, are usually done by students, recent graduates, or paralegals. The same holds true for most cases of uncontested divorce and probate, home closings, appraisals, simple incorporations and bankruptcies, and other common affairs.

**3.** *"If your secretary or staff does most of the work on my case, will my bill be less?"* Why should you pay the lawyer's hourly fees for what is mostly clerical work? Press this point.

***Are you paying for legal or secretarial work?***

If lawyers actually do work on your case, the standardized forms that are completed and filed by secretaries save them considerable expense. But many lawyers neglect to pass these savings on to their clients in the form of lower costs. Find out if the lawyer you interview is among them.

The expedience of standardized forms, and the realization that secretaries and paralegals perform considerable "legal" work supposedly reserved for lawyers, led to the establishment of storefront legal clinics and other high volume legal businesses. They can perform routine legal services competently. You go to a conventional lawyer or firm for more "individual" attention. If you are not going to get it, try another lawyer—or go to a clinic.

**4.** The American Bar Association has established suggested guidelines for law office management, but practices vary from lawyer to lawyer. Still, you may wish to ask for a copy of any guidelines the office has and ask questions about what guidelines, if any, the office follows. You want to know how a lawyer manages an office, bills clients, delegates work, uses standard forms, etc.

*Be sure to ask specific questions about billing practices.* How will you be billed and for what? Lawyers usually bill by the tenth or quarter of an hour. If the lawyer charges, for instance, $75 per hour, a three minute phone conversation will cost you $7.50 (if billed to the tenth of an hour) *or* $18.75 (if billed to

***How will you be billed?***

the quarter hour). The same holds for visits and writing letters. *Get a detailed description from the lawyer about this,* and make sure that you understand it *clearly.*

***Will there be additional costs?***

Ask also about the variety of additional costs that will accumulate. Secretarial fees, court costs, filing fees, etc., add up very quickly. Xeroxing costs can be expensive (lawyers charge notoriously high prices for copying). Still, it is important that you have copies of *essential* letters and documents written on your behalf.

Some lawyers require a "retainer" before they will work for you. In common language that means a downpayment. If you pay one, get a receipt. Request a periodic billing with itemizations balanced against the retainer until it is gone. Insist that you receive an itemized bill *at least once a month.*

***Get an estimate for all charges.***

**5.** *"What are your fee arrangements?"* Ask frankly what the lawyer's charges are and exactly how the charges are figured. The lawyer should be able and willing to provide an estimate of your bill which includes services and costs and any additional charges that may arise. Ask for a projection of costs that includes a breakdown of all charges: lawyer's fees, filing fees, court costs, charges for letters, phone calls, documents, depositions, xeroxing, and other additional costs. Does the lawyer require a "retainer?" How much is required and how are charges balanced against it?

Various fee arrangements and payment schedules are possible. The exact form these arrangements may take depends upon the location, the lawyer, the nature of the work to be done, and your financial situation. The different types of fee arrangements are discussed in Section V.

***Get a signed time-table.***

**6.** *"Can you give me an idea how long it will take to complete this matter?"* Find out what steps are to be taken, what occurs with each one, and how long each takes. Insist that the lawyer draft, sign, and give you a copy of a written time-table. The time-table is a must if you have agreed upon an hourly fee arrangement. It should help prevent the lawyer from protracting a matter unnecessarily to increase the fee. *Do not* settle for a vague estimate of time and costs in the time-table. Find out exactly what the estimate depends upon. And get a clear idea of 1) the *period* of time that will be required to resolve the matter, and 2) the extent of the *lawyer's actual time* required for the matter. At the very least, get an estimate expressing the possible range of costs and establish a maximum allowable fee.

**7.** *"How involved are your clients in your conduct of their legal affairs?"* It's important that a lawyer understand your situation. Attitudes toward cooperation and client involvement are even more important.

What is the lawyer's policy towards working with clients? Have they been kept directly involved in the conduct of their affairs? Will *you* be kept informed and involved? How? Ask if you can speak with the lawyer's other clients about this.

Even if you are too busy to work directly with the lawyer on everything, you will want the lawyer to be accessible at times that are convenient or important to you. And you will want to stay informed. Clarify when the two of you will communicate and how you will cooperate.

***How will you participate in the case?***

There is no point to badgering a lawyer: remember, you'll be charged for every minute. But it will be *your* affairs that the lawyer works on. It is your responsibility, and right, to know what goes on and what is done at every point. The more directly you remain involved, the less likely it is that you will be surprised by unexpected developments. Incomplete or incompetent work by the lawyer, additional costs creeping into the bill, and astonishing fees for routine services will not surface unexpectedly.

A client should not "dump" everything into a lawyer's lap, however trustworthy the lawyer. Stay involved. Work cooperatively with a lawyer, but do not become entirely dependent upon one.

***8.*** *"What if something goes wrong, or if we disagree about your handling of this matter?"* You are seeking a lawyer's training and advice, but you will pay for it and *your* interests are at stake. That makes you the boss. You can "fire" a lawyer whenever you please.

Still, you want to avoid this. It's frustrating to change horses in midstream. You may already have a large bill, and would have to start from scratch with another lawyer. It could also jeopardize your case if you can't obtain an adequate delay from the court.

Thus it's vital to discuss how disagreements will be handled. The lawyer must understand from the beginning that you are in control. It will help to keep communications open and to prevent misunderstandings. And if you stay involved, it's unlikely that anything will go wrong without your knowing about it. Recognizing problems as they arise will make it easier to straighten things out quickly, or to change lawyers, or to handle things yourself if necessary.

***What if there's a disagreement?***

Of course, if the lawyer does botch everything, you want to know what compensations there will be. Will you have to pay full fees, or merely costs? Ask for an explanation of bar association grievance and fee arbitration procedures. Will the lawyer submit, if there are problems, to independent arbitration by a body other than the bar association? Submission of disputes by both parties to arbitration must be included in the original written agreement. If it is omitted, there is little you can do once a dispute arises.

Face this issue bluntly. It occurs all too frequently. Get something in writing that makes provisions for the lawyer's mishandling of your affairs—before you hire anyone.

These questions should help you get a clear idea about the practices and the attitudes to look for in any lawyer that you interview. Undoubtedly, other questions will arise. Ask them and make sure you get straightforward answers. Keep notes on the responses you get. Think about them, discuss them with friends, and compare them to the responses of other lawyers. The comparisons will help you narrow the field of available candidates to a final choice.

# V. ABOUT FEES

Most people understand one thing about lawyer's fees: however they are figured, they are too high. One reason for the high level of legal fees is the monopoly that lawyers hold over legal services. They can set fees arbitrarily, and have the power to prevent others from offering competent services at lower prices.

***There are three basic fee arrangements.***

Before dealing with a lawyer, you should know something about their basic fee arrangements. These are the *flat fee,* the *hourly rate,* and the *contingency fee* arrangement. Combinations of these three, and individual arrangements, are also possible.

**FLAT FEE.** The "flat fee," or set charge for a specific job, is a common fee arrangement. It is used for those legal matters that arise often: wills, probate, divorce, title searches and property transfers, etc. Most of these matters are simple enough that a routine procedure can be established for a set charge. The same principle is the basis for high volume legal clinics. The main difference between the clinic and the individual lawyer's service is that the lawyer's set charge will probably be significantly higher.

Flat fees vary considerably between individual lawyers. The charge will depend upon locale, upon the lawyer's experience and reputation, and upon the lawyer's degree of "specialization."

***The flat fee applies only for routine legal matters.***

The flat fee is the easiest charge to check and compare. Simply call several lawyers to ask what their fees are for the specific job you have in mind. Be sure to check out what additional costs can be tacked onto an advertised or quoted flat fee. Often, even the slightest departure from routine handling will result in extra charges. The flat fee offer should be scrutinized to determine what work will be covered and what will not. Call a clinic or other high volume business for a comparison of both flat fees and the cost of additional services.

Set fees for specific jobs are sometimes charged in the form of percentages. The lawyer will perform the legal tasks for a percentage of the amount of money or value of property involved. This is common in probate. A lawyer may be allowed by local probate law to take, for example, a flat 10% of the estate for a fee. The percentage varies from place to place. Of course, the percentage does *not* include various additional costs, expenses, and extra services that the lawyer deems necessary.

Percentage fees for these routine legal tasks are an inequitable way of figuring charges. For instance, in probating an estate, it takes a lawyer no more time or effort to transfer 500 shares of stock than 5 shares. A simple phone call or letter does the trick for both. Yet the 10% of the former transaction that goes into the lawyer's pocket is substantially higher although it involves an equivalent amount of "work." Such a fee arrangement has little, if any, relation to the amount of work performed or the legal skill required to do it.

***Percentage fees are seldom based on the work involved.***

**HOURLY.** Hourly rates are the most common type of fee that lawyers charge. The fee is computed on a straight per hour basis: the hourly rate multiplied by the number of hours the lawyer spends on your case or matter.

The hourly rate varies with different regions of the country, and with individual lawyers. It can range from $15 to $200 per hour, and higher. The location and size of a firm, the seniority or experience of the lawyer, the complexity of the problem, and the "competition" in the area all enter into the setting of lawyers' hourly rates.

Remember: you will be charged for all work by the *tenth* or *quarter* hour. Five minutes on the phone with your lawyer may mean a bill to you for fifteen minutes. Remember, too, that the hourly fee does not include the various expenses and additional costs that accumulate in every case.

***Hourly fees are billed in large increments of an hour.***

Lawyers for hire at an hourly rate may request a "retainer" (i.e., a downpayment). Usually, a retainer represents a certain amount of the lawyer's time at the normal rate. If the lawyer's time on your affairs exceeds the amount paid for in advance, you will get billed for additional charges. If the lawyer spends less time than the retainer covers, you should get a refund.

If you put down a payment, get a receipt. Request periodic billings, with itemizations balanced against the retainer, so you'll know when, and if, your retainer coverage is exhausted.

**CONTINGENCY FEES.** Under a *contingency fee* arrangement, you pay a lawyer only if your case is won. The lawyer's fee is "contingent" or dependent on the case being won and a financial award being made. If the case is lost, the lawyer receives no fee. (Court costs and the lawyer's out-of-pocket expenses, however, may have to be paid by you whatever the outcome of the case.)

***Contingency fees are paid only if you win the case.***

The contingency fee arrangement is supposed to benefit persons who have valid legal claims but lack the financial means to endure lengthy litigation while employing a lawyer on an hourly fee basis. A lawyer who accepts a case "on contingency" agrees to represent a client for a fee that will be calculated as a percentage of whatever financial award is obtained when the matter is settled. This arrangement is common in personal injury, workman's compensation, and wrongful death cases.

***Contingency fees are a percentage of the settlement.***

The exact percentage of the final settlement award that a lawyer can claim as a fee should be negotiated in your attorney employment contract (see page 17 and the Appendix). Contingency fee arrangements can vary from 5% to 60% of the final award, depending on the lawyer, the circumstances of the case, and the chances of obtaining a favorable judgment. The "customary" arrangement that most lawyers ask for is usually around one-third (33.3%) of the final settlement award.

Cases taken on contingency are frequently settled out of court. A negotiated settlement may be reached during the course of the trial or even before a trial begins. In these cases, the actual settlement is usually less than the amount originally claimed. A true contingency fee binds the attorney's percentage to the *actual* amount of the award. If you receive less money, the attorney receives a smaller fee.

One common way of allowing contingency fee arrangements to account for out-of-court settlements is to set a "sliding fee scale" with the attorney before the case begins. For example, if the case is settled before a lawsuit is filed, the lawyer might be guaranteed 15% of the settlement. If the case is settled after filing, the lawyer might be given 20%. If the case is settled after the trial begins but before the court makes a decision, the lawyer might be given 25%. If a complete trial is necessary, the lawyer might receive 33% of the amount awarded.

***Set a sliding fee scale.***

Remember that unless your attorney employment contract states otherwise, the lawyer is paid a percentage of the *entire* settlement or award. The court costs and other expenses will be paid out of your remaining portion of the award.

The rationale used to justify the contingency fee is that is it encourages lawyers to take cases, at a calculated risk, for people who could not otherwise afford to seek recovery for damages or suffering caused by others. But in many cases taken on contingency, there is little or no risk that there will not be a settlement. There are many attorneys who will handle routine contingency cases on an hourly fee basis, and some will even offer special financing arrangements for pre-trial costs if necessary. Other attorneys will accept a percentage that is much lower than the "customary" percentage rates if it is obvious that a settlement from, for example, an insurance company is certain.

***Seek alternatives to "customary" contingency fees.***

On the whole, the contingency fee is a questionable arrangement. You should always explore the alternative fee arrangements that are available in your community (*i.e.,* hourly arrangements or special financing) *before* you sign a contingency fee contract. You should accept a contingency arrangement only if you are in real financial hardship, or if you cannot raise the money to hire a lawyer on an hourly basis, or if the chances of winning (or collecting) an award are relatively slim. When the contingency arrangement is your only option, be skeptical of the "customary" fees quoted by lawyers. You may be able to hire a competent attorney for a much smaller percentage of your potential award if you are willing to shop around and negotiate the fee.

*'Minimum fee schedules' are illegal.*

Before 1975, local bar associations commonly set "minimum fee schedules." No lawyer who belonged to the bar could offer services below the minimum fee. Of course, every lawyer had to belong to the bar in order to practice law. It was a convenient method of price-fixing, and prohibited the emergence of a competitive market in legal services.

In 1975, the U.S. Supreme Court struck down the formal practice of setting minimum fee schedules, which it called anti-competitive price-fixing (*Goldfarb v. The Virginia State Bar Association*). However, in many areas informal agreements between lawyers still exist which effectively establish minimum fees. This informal practice is under government investigation in some cases, and the Supreme Court's decision eventually may serve as a precedent for challenging percentage fees and the bar's monopoly over routine "legal" services.

**Negotiate a final price.**

Remember, too, that prices set forth by informal bar association guidelines do not have to be the final word on fees. Many lawyers will bargain for their fees or negotiate a special arrangement. You don't have to accept the first fee mentioned. Bargain over the cost of a lawyer's services in the same way you would over the cost of a used car. You could ask for a breakdown of the fee estimate, and not hesitate to point out that similar services are available elsewhere at lower cost.

# VI. THE FINAL CHOICE

When you have interviewed several lawyers, and have considered their various qualities, attitudes, and fees, you must make a final choice. Review the questions you asked individual lawyers. Recall the responses you received, and the attitudes expressed. What did you learn of what's to be involved in your case or legal matter? How do the estimated fees and costs compare? Who do you think *you* can work with comfortably?

Discuss all these things with friends or relatives. And consider one more time whether you have the alternative of settling your dispute or of managing

*Before you choose, review the alternatives.*

your legal affairs by other means. Review the alternatives:

***1.*** *Can you* resolve things or handle matters entirely on your own? An honest and cooperative discussion may settle a dispute. An experienced friend may know all the ropes. Procedural manuals and standard forms may be all you need.

***2.*** Can you obtain the professional advice you need simply, quickly, and inexpensively? Law schools, community groups, or non-lawyer professionals may have the information you need, or be able to suggest other alternatives. A lawyer might agree to act as your advisor at a lower rate than usual.

***3.*** Can a government agency, a public interest group, or a professional arbitrator help you resolve or manage things without a lawyer?

***4.*** Can you obtain free public legal assistance?

***5.*** Can a legal clinic or other high volume legal business competently provide all the service you require?

In the end, the final choice is yours—alone. But if you have been diligent, you are now equipped with as much relevant information as can be gathered to help you make the decision. And you are fully aware of some lawyers' tricks. You know that you require a specific service, not some mysterious ritual performed in an obscure or secret language.

# VII. SEALING THE DEAL

You've selected a lawyer. The choice was carefully made on the basis of information collected in interviews, and comparisons with other providers of legal services. Now make sure that your reasons for selecting a particular lawyer become the actual basis for the client-lawyer relationship.

*Get a written billing agreement.*

Establish a written *fee and payment schedule* that you understand clearly. Be specific about billings, and insist that the lawyer do the same. Depending upon the services you require, *demand regular billings* by the specific job, by the month, or by the accumulation of a certain amount due. You can insist that the lawyer *not* exceed a certain number of hours, or a certain limit to fees and costs, without obtaining your permission.

*Demand a monthly itemized bill.*

*Insist* that all billings be *specific:* have all charges for time, fees, costs, activities, and expenses *itemized*. If there is a downpayment (retainer) involved, get a receipt and request a running balance of charges against it. Unless instructed otherwise, many lawyers will send a monthly or quarterly "summary of services performed." This is meant to include everything and is presented as a lump sum. *Do not* accept it. *Insist* upon itemization of date, time, number of hours involved, *and* indication of who actually did the work. Keep your own organized records of billings, and of all meetings, conversations, and the activities of the lawyer.

Put this arrangement with the lawyer *in writing*. It will be your contract. It should set forth the lawyer's fee schedule and costs, and the services to be performed. It should include *all* verbal agreements and arrangements that you discussed when interviewing the lawyer. It should lay out the lawyer's proposed strategy for a case, and subject it to *your* veto or modification. And it should make some provision for dealing with difficulties. Also find out if you will be charged for time spent in drawing up your employment agreement. If so, agree on the charge beforehand. A lawyer who doesn't charge for this is demonstrating his regard for your rights as a client. You may choose to use this factor as a criterion in making a final decision on the lawyer you want to hire. For further information on attorney employment contracts, see the Appendix.

***Get all agreements in writing.***

Have *two copies* of the contract made: one for the lawyer and one for your own records. You and the lawyer should sign *both* copies. Perhaps you can have a friend witness the signing. But *do not* sign *anything* until you *fully* understand what it means, and unless it contains all the arrangements you have agreed upon. In the event of a dispute, this written agreement will be presumed to constitute the *entire* agreement. Thus make sure that *all* understandings are included.

# VIII. PROBLEMS AFTERWARDS?

Remember: *you* are the boss. You have the right to fire your lawyer when services are not performed as promised. If the lawyer does not keep you informed and involved, or send you regular billings, or stick to the timetable, or conform to other provisions of the contract, it may be time to make a change.

As mentioned earlier, however, you don't want to fire a lawyer unnecessarily. You may already have a large bill which will have to be paid even if you dismiss the lawyer. You may have difficulty obtaining another lawyer, especially if the first one was known and respected in the legal community. And your case may have reached a critical stage that cannot be delayed.

Before making any decision about dismissal, discuss the situation with the lawyer. Perhaps the problem is due to a misunderstanding or to a lack of communication.

***If there are problems, refer to your contract.***

If you have any reason to discuss the lawyer's handling of your case, or to challenge a billing, it should be understood that the 'meter is *not* running' at your expense while doing this. *State* beforehand that you expect there to be no charge for this particular communication. Refer to the contract, and try to resolve the difficulties. If provisions were made for such a situation in the contract, a resolution might be easier. If these steps do not work, then you should probably change lawyers, or seek assistance elsewhere.

If the lawyer really botched things, or behaved unethically, you can file a complaint with the local bar association. Most bar associations maintain a standing committee to review client complaints. The committee will investigate the matter, and recommend to the bar association whether any disciplinary action or judgment against the lawyer is necessary. Many bar associations also have a "fee arbitration" committee to settle disputes over fees only.

***Bar association committees: Can they help?***

Most of these bar association committees are dominated by lawyers. The fact that lawyers are supposed to judge complaints against professional, and occasionally social, acquaintances has spurred critics to call these committees ineffectual arrangements. In addition, critics charge that these committees consider only a small percentage of the complaints they receive. Nevertheless, there is a national trend towards increased public (i.e. non-lawyer) participation in and scrutiny of bar association regulatory bodies. As a result, a well-organized complaint presented to a bar committee with at least some non-lawyer members is more likely to obtain serious consideration today than ever before.

***Arrange in your contract for independent arbitration.***

Of course, you may have provided in the agreement with your lawyer for truly independent arbitration of any disputes. This would mean submitting the difficulty to an arbitration body (other than the bar) for final resolution. It will not be easy to get a lawyer to agree to this ahead of time, but it is in your best interests. Another alternative is to submit a claim to a small claims court for recovery of money spent for services that were not rendered.

Keep in mind that all of these steps apply only to your dissatisfaction with the *quality* or *competence* of services performed by the lawyer, or with the fact that fees are higher than agreed upon. *Results* can be a different matter altogether, as long as the lawyer has completed the proper work responsibly. Only if the lawyer behaved irresponsibly do you have grounds for contesting fees and even for challenging the lawyer's professional standing.

# Conclusion

Across the country, many people have recognized the terrible financial and psychological burdens of "legalism." Lawyers, with obscure language and overcomplicated procedures, have woven legal webs around nearly every aspect of private, business, and public life. The search for alternatives to lawyers and legalism has begun.

Citizen groups have banded together to create centers for dispute resolution. More and more people are attempting to handle their own legal affairs. The use of arbitration is increasing. Reforms are being promoted to simplify legal procedures. Legislation has been introduced in Congress to streamline the courts, and to develop less expensive legal services.

When managing your own legal affairs, search within the community to discover alternatives to expensive lawyers and court procedures. When you must make use of conventional legal measures, learn from the experience of others, and lend your support and advice to those who find themselves in a similar situation.

The law has become remote, mysterious, and intimidating to American citizens even in its most routine civil applications. The dependence of citizens upon lawyers, and of lawyers upon overcomplicated procedures, have been major reasons for this. The first step in clearing away the general ignorance of citizens about our legal system, and in lifting the veil of mystery which shrouds it, is for citizens to take a more active role in the conduct of their own legal affairs.

## For Further "Shopping" Information:

Consumer Reports. "How To Choose A Good Lawyer." Consumer Reports 42:284. May 1977.

Denenberg, Herbert S. *The Shopper's Guidebook.* Consumer News, Inc.: Washington, D.C. 1974.

Jervis, Bruce M. *How To Choose The Right Lawyer.* Novation Publishing Company: Portland, Maine. 1978.

Kahan, Stuart. *Do I Really Need A Lawyer?* Chilton Book Company: Radnor, Pennsylvania. 1979.

McGinn, Joseph C. *A Client's Manual.* Prentice-Hall, Inc.: Englewood Cliffs, N.J. 1979.

Schweitzer, S.C. "How To Pick A Lawyer." 50 Plus, 19:32-33. February, 1979.

Shapiro, A.O. "How To Shop For A Lawyer." New Yorker, 12:65-66. March 12, 1979.

Smith, Gregory White, and Naifeh, Steven, *What Every Client Needs To Know About Using A Lawyer.* G.P. Putnam's Sons: New York, N.Y. 1982.

Wehringer, Cameron K. *When and How to Choose an Attorney.* Oceana Publications, Inc.: Dobbs Ferry, New York. 1970.

## For General Information:

Rodell, Fred. *Woe Unto You, Lawyers!* Berkeley Books, N.Y. 1980-81.

Bloom, Murray Teigh. *The Trouble With Lawyers.* Simon and Schuster: New York. 1968.

Coulson, Robert. *How To Stay Out of Court.* Award Books: New York. 1968.

Golde, Roger A. *Can You Be Sure of Your Experts?* Macmillan Co.: New York. 1969.

Landsman, Stephen. McWherter, Donald. Pfeffer, Alan. *What To Do Until The Lawyer Comes.* Anchor Press/Doubleday: New York. 1977.

Mayer, Martin. *How To Think Of Lawyers And The Law.* Dreyfus Publishing: New York. 1973.

McGinn, Joseph C. *A Client's Manual.* Prentice-Hall, Inc.: Englewood Cliffs, N.J. 1979.

Menzel, Harold H. *How To Deal With Lawyers.* Real World Publishing: Longmont, Colorado. 1976.

Reader's Digest. *You and the Law.* The Reader's Digest Association, Inc.: Pleasantville, New York. 1971.

Rice, Jerome S. *How To Handle Your Own Lawsuit.* Contemporary Books, Inc.: Chicago, Illinois. 1979.

Rosenthal, Douglas E. *Lawyer & Client: Who's In Charge?* Transaction Books: New Jersey. 1974.

Siegel, Edward. *How To Avoid Lawyers.* Hawthorne Books. New York. 1969.

Simons, Blaine N. *Games Lawyers Play With Your Money.* Condor Publishing Company, Inc.: New York. 1978.

# APPENDIX
## Attorney Employment Contracts

Many attorneys now offer a standard one-page retainer agreement for their clients to sign. The principal reason for this short-form contract is the fear that a longer contract will merely intimidate a potential client. This fear, plus the fact that the primary focus of the document is often the client's agreement to pay, makes these forms necessarily incomplete.

The following contract was designed to secure the rights and stipulate the responsibilities of both the attorney and his client. It is also meant to serve as a discussion document by which the client may learn enough about a particular attorney's business practices to make an informed choice as a consumer of legal services.

Use of the following contract (or a modified version of it) is of course a decision to be made entirely by the client and his attorney. However, HALT's research has shown that most disputes between clients and their attorneys could have been avoided if the nature of their relationship had been made explicit at the outset. If your attorney refuses to sign or draft a document such as this, ask for his reasons. His answers will tell you whether or not he is the sort of attorney you want to employ.

The contract printed in full below is an agreement to employ an attorney on an hourly fee basis. For contingent or fixed fee arrangements, replace Section One—Attorney's Fees—of the hourly fee contract with the appropriate Section One (Contingent or Fixed), which follows the full contract.

# CONTRACT TO EMPLOY ATTORNEY

__________ *(name)* (referred to in this contract as Client) of __________ *(address)* requests and authorizes __________ *(name)* (referred to in this contract as Attorney) of __________ *(name of Firm)* at __________ *(address)* to represent Client as his/her Attorney in fact and in law as related to

SPECIFIC DESCRIPTION OF NATURE AND EXTENT OF CASE

(e.g., 'a divorce proceeding between X and Y for which Attorney will conduct negotiations and make court appearances which are necessary to securing separation, custody, property, and dissolution agreements, including a final decree, but not including an appeal')

and against all additional persons, firms, or corporations who may appear to be related to this case.

## SECTION ONE
### Attorney's Fees

Compensation for Attorney's services shall be based on an hourly fee arrangement.

(1) Client will pay Attorney the sum of __________Dollars ($______) per hour for Attorney's time spent in research, writing, consultation, conference with opposing parties, and other matters specifically related to the case described above.

(2) Attorney's additional charges (if any) for appearances in court are as follows:

| | | |
|---|---|---|
| Routine appearances (e.g., motions for continuances) | $______ | per ______ |
| Simple motions (e.g., for temporary custody, discovery motions, etc.) | $______ | per ______ |
| Trials or Hearings | $______ | per ______ |

(3) If a junior partner, associate, or staff attorney within the Firm performs research or other services for the Client, the Client will pay for those services at the rate of __________Dollars ($______) per hour. Any court appearance of junior member of the firm will be charged to the Client at a rate of ______percent (______%) of the court appearance charges of the Attorney, as given in I(1) above.

(4) For all services performed by paralegals for the Client, the Client will pay for those services at the rate of __________Dollars ($______) per hour.

(5) If Client is to be charged for secretarial services, Client will pay for those services at the rate of __________ Dollars ($______) per hour.

(6) Time charges will be computed and billed to the tenth of an hour.

(7) It is necessary to incur certain court costs in order to successfully complete this case. Client agrees to pay for all additional court costs at the following *rates:*

| | | |
|---|---|---|
| ☐ Filing Fees | $______ | per ______ |
| ☐ Deposition fees | $______ | per ______ |

(7) *Continued:*

- ☐ Fees for Court Reporter $________ per ________
- ☐ Charges for Transcripts $________ per ________
- ☐ Subpoena fees $________ per ________
- ☐ Fees for expert witnesses $________ per ________

(8) Attorney estimates that these court costs will not exceed the sum of ______________Dollars ($________).
(9) Client also agrees to pay for any of the additional costs checked below at the following *rates:*

- ☐ Charges for local phone calls $________ per ________
- ☐ Charges for postage (e.g., registered mail) $________ per ________
- ☐ Long distance phone charges ________% of STD. RATE
- ☐ Document search and file (including computer time) $________ per ________
- ☐ Special research or Investigation (e.g., a private investigator) $________ per ________
- ☐ Travel $________ per ________
- ☐ Other: ______________________________ $________________

(10) Attorney estimates additional costs listed in (9) above will not exceed the sum of ______________Dollars ($________).
(11) Attorney shall pay all of his own personal and travel expenses incurred within the (county) (city) of ______________.
(12) The total estimated number of hours required for the completion of this case are as follows: ________ hours by Attorney; ________ hours by junior members of firm; and ________ hours by paralegals.
(13) Attorney estimates that the total cost of fees for the services of Attorney, junior members, and paralegals will not exceed the sum of ______________Dollars ($________).
(14) Client will not be liable for any additional costs or fees which exceed the estimates given in I(8), I(10), and I(13) unless Attorney notifies Client of the additional expenses required and receives permission of Client *prior* to actually incurring the additional expenses.
(15) (OPTIONAL) The total cost of completing this case shall not under any circumstances exceed the estimates given in I(8), I(10), and I(13) by a factor of ________percent (________%). [NOTE: For certain cases, there may be several unknown factors at the outset—e.g., whether or not the opposing party will decide to litigate or settle. Therefore, it may be necessary for Attorney and Client to set spending limits which are conditional upon certain events. For example, both "If the case is settled without litigation, the total cost..., etc." *and* "If litigation is required to settle the case, ..." may be necessary.]

## SECTION TWO
### Billing Agreement

(1) Client will not be billed for Attorney's time in the preparation or discussion of this employment contract. Secretarial time may be charged for the preparation of the original document and copies (this charge is to be included in the estimate of additional costs).
(2) Client will pay a retainer of ______________Dollars ($________) and receive a signed receipt from the Attorney for said amount.
(3) Client will receive a statement with detailed itemization of the Attorney's, junior members' and paralegals' activities in the case; the amount of time involved; and the additional costs incurred. This statement will be sent to the Client on a monthly (or other ______________) basis and/or per unit of expenditure (e.g., each time the bill increases by $250, an up-dated statement is to be sent). If per unit billing is adopted, that unit will be ______________Dollars ($________).
(4) All costs and expenses are to be deducted (unless otherwise noted) from the retainer. The current balance of the client's retainer is to be plainly indicated in each itemized statement.
(5) The Attorney's fees (may) (may not) be deducted from the retainer.
(6) The Client is to be notified in writing prior to the depletion of the retainer.
(7) Should the retainer exceed the total cost of completing the case, the remainder is to be returned in full to the Client.
(8) Should the cost of conducting the case exceed the retainer but not the estimate or agreed maximum, the Client agrees to reimburse the Attorney for the additional costs and/but not (delete one) the Attorney's fees within ______________(________) days of receipt of an itemized statement.
(9) If the total cost exceeds the retainer but not the agreed maximum, payment for outstanding fees and costs upon completion of the case shall be by (a lump sum payment) (payment in full within thirty (30) days of submission of a properly itemized statement) (monthly payments of ______________Dollars ($________)).
(10) Attorney shall receive no other compensation in any manner or form than that provided for expressly by this agreement.

# SECTION THREE
## Attorney's Rights And Responsibilities

(1) This contract represents earnest compliance with Ethical Consideration 2-19 of the American Bar Association's Code of Professional Responsibility. Attorney consents to be bound by all Canons, Ethical Considerations, and Disciplinary Rules of the ABA Code as amended August 10, 1977.
(2) Violation of any provision within the ABA Code or any agreement within this contract of employment shall be grounds for dismissal of the Attorney.
(3) As mandated by the ABA Code, the Attorney shall regularly inform the Client of progress (if any) in the Client's case. This shall include copies of pleadings, briefs, memorandums, and relevant correspondence as the case progresses.
(4) The Attorney shall freely and frankly discuss the strategy and progress of the case with the Client upon request. The Attorney must consult and seek permission of the Client before taking any action which may significantly affect the outcome or cost of the proceedings.
(5) The Attorney may not under any circumstances agree to settle a case without the prior consent of the Client.
(6) Withdrawal from representation by Attorney is mandatory upon discharge by Client.

# SECTION FOUR
## Client's Rights And Responsibilities

(1) Client agrees to truthfully disclose all relevant information to Attorney upon request.
(2) Client will make himself (or herself) and any documents, persons, or things under the Client's control available to the Attorney at reasonable times and places for such conferences, inspections, discussions, and legal proceedings as may be necessary from time to time.
(3) Client will promptly notify the Attorney of any change in the Client's address or phone number.
(4) In an effort to increase client participation and to reduce costs, Client will (at the direction of the Attorney) perform these tasks:

(E.G., LOCATING EVIDENCE, CONTACTING WITNESSES,
FILING DOCUMENTS WITH COURT CLERK, ETC.)

(5) Failure of Client to seek counsel of Attorney before taking any action which may affect the course or resolution of the case represents sufficient grounds for Attorney withdrawing from employment.
(6) Attorney may not withdraw from employment unless (i) the Client receives fourteen (14) days notice prior to withdrawal, (ii) withdrawal will not significantly affect the outcome of imminent proceedings; and (iii), competent counsel may be readily obtained elsewhere by Client.
(7) The Attorney may not condition completion of representation of Client upon payment of estimated or actual fee under any terms other than those stipulated within this contract.
(8) All documents presented by Client to Attorney remain the exclusive property of Client and must be returned upon demand. Attorney expressly relinquishes all general, possessory, or retaining liens known to the common or statutory law.
(9) It is further agreed that:

# SECTION FIVE
## Disputes

(1) Attorney and Client recognize the benefits of maintaining a harmonious working relationship. Both agree to openly discuss any cause of dissatisfaction and to seek reconciliation.
(2) Should either party believe itself to be seriously wronged or believe that the terms of this contract have been substantially violated, resolution shall be sought through binding arbitration by a third party mutually agreed to by both Attorney and Client.

# SECTION SIX
## Disclaimer of Warranty

No warranties have been made by Attorney with respect to the successful termination of this case. All expressions made by Attorney about the possible outcome of the case are matters of Attorney's opinion only.

## SECTION SEVEN
### Notice

Any notices required under this agreement shall be in writing and shall be deemed to have been duly served if delivered in person, or if delivered at or sent by first class mail to the business address of the person for whom it is intended, as specified in this agreement.

## SECTION EIGHT
### Law To Govern Contract

The laws of the State of ______________ shall govern the construction and interpretation of this agreement.

## SECTION NINE

This contract is valid only with regard to the case described above. An appeal of this case to a higher court, or a re-trial before a similar court will require a separate employment contract.

This contract has been read, understood, signed, and attested to on this day, ______________, 19________, by the undersigned.

ATTORNEY(S) ______________________________ CLIENT(S) ______________________________

______________________________ ______________________________

______________________________ ______________________________

WITNESS ______________________________

---

***For A Contingent Fee Arrangement:***

## SECTION ONE
### Attorney's Fees

Compensation for Attorney's services shall be based on a contingent fee arrangement.

(1) The contingent fee shall be based on a percentage of the actual recovery, *after* all expenses indicated in I(3) and (5) below have been deducted.

(2) The contingent fee rate will be determined as follows. If the case is settled:

a. Before the case is filed in court, ______________percent (________%).
b. After the case is filed in court, ______________percent (________%).
c. After the trial begins, but before a decision by the court, ______________percent (________%).
d. At conclusion of trial, by a decision of the court, ______________percent (________%).

(3) It is necessary to incur certain court costs in order to successfully complete this case. Client agrees to pay for all additional court costs at the following *rates:*

☐ Filing Fees $________ per ________
☐ Deposition fees $________ per ________
☐ Fees for Court Reporter $________ per ________
☐ Charges for Transcripts $________ per ________
☐ Subpoena fees $________ per ________
☐ Fees for expert witnesses $________ per ________

(4) Attorney estimates that these court costs will not exceed the sum of ______________Dollars ($________).

(5) Client also agrees to pay for any of the additional costs checked below at the following *rates:*

☐ Charges for local phone calls $________ per ________
☐ Charges for postage (e.g., registered mail) $________ per ________
☐ Long distance phone charges ________% of STD. RATE
☐ Document search and file (including computer time) $________ per ________
☐ Special research or Investigation (e.g., a private investigator) $________ per ________
☐ Travel $________ per ________
☐ Other: ______________________________ $________________

(6) Attorney estimates additional costs listed in (5) above will not exceed the sum of ______________Dollars ($________).

(7) Attorney shall pay all of his own personal and travel expenses incurred within the (county) (city) of ______________.

(8) The total estimated additional costs required for the completion of this case are $________. If the case is settled before a decision of the court, these additional costs will be reduced accordingly.

(9) Client may be requested to advance in part or in full the funds required to meet these costs. If so, this pre-payment is designated as the 'retainer' in Section Two (below).

(10) Client will not be liable for any additional costs which exceed the estimate given in I(8) unless the Attorney notifies the Client of the additional expenses required and receives permission of Client *prior* to actually incurring the additional expenses.

(11) (OPTIONAL) The total additional costs and expenses incurred in completing this case shall not under any circumstances exceed the estimate given in I(8) by a factor of 20%.

(12) If the case is lost, Client is liable only for the costs incurred, within the limits determined by I(8) and I(11) (if applicable). Client is also liable for opponent's costs, should the court so decide.

(13) The decision to appeal against the verdict of the court is the exclusive right of the client.

(14) Attorney is (given) (denied) a special or charging lien on the claim or cause of action, on any sum recovered by way of settlement, and on any judgement that may be recovered, for the sum mentioned above as his fee. That is, Client (is) (is not) free to use any portion of the recovery for his own purposes until Attorney is first reimbursed for his fee.

(15) Costs and expenses incurred by Attorney in advancing Client's cause are to be borne by Client. All costs which are not covered by funds advanced by Client to Attorney will be (paid by Client in periodic billings) (advanced by Attorney, with reimbursement to be made from the gross proceeds of any recovery, which reimbursements shall be in addition to the percentage fee).

(16) If Client settles his claim without consent of Attorney, Client will pay to Attorney his fee computed in accordance with the terms of this agreement and based on the final recovery received by Client in his settlement, and Client will reimburse Attorney for all advances made for costs and other expenses.

***For A Fixed Fee Arrangement:***

## SECTION ONE
### Attorney's Fees

Compensation of Attorney's services shall be based on a fixed fee arrangement.

(1) Client will pay Attorney the sum of ______________Dollars ($________) as full reimbursement for the completion of all services required to conclude and resolve all aspects of the case described above.

(2) The fixed fee amount given in I(1) above does not include any of the additional costs checked below. Client agrees to pay for all additional court costs at the following *rates:*

- ☐ Filing Fees $________ per ________
- ☐ Deposition fees $________ per ________
- ☐ Fees for Court Reporter $________ per ________
- ☐ Charges for Transcripts $________ per ________
- ☐ Subpoena fees $________ per ________
- ☐ Fees for expert witnesses $________ per ________

(3) Attorney estimates that these court costs will not exceed the sum of ______________Dollars ($________).

(4) Client also agrees to pay for any of the additional costs checked below at the following *rates:*

- ☐ Charges for local phone calls $________ per ________
- ☐ Charges for postage (e.g., registered mail) $________ per ________
- ☐ Long distance phone charges ________% of STD. RATE
- ☐ Document search and file (including computer time) $________ per ________
- ☐ Special research or Investigation (e.g., a private investigator) $________ per ________
- ☐ Travel $________ per ________
- ☐ Other: ________________________ $________________

(5) Attorney estimates additional costs listed in (4) above will not exceed the sum of ______________Dollars ($________).

(6)Attorney shall pay all of his own personal and travel expenses incurred within the (county) (city) of ______________.

(7) Time charges for any of the additional costs checked above will be computed and billed to the tenth of an hour.

(8) Client will not be liable for any additional costs which exceed the estimate given in I(8) unless the Attorney notifies the Client of the additional expense required and receives permission of Client *prior* to actually incurring the additional costs.

(10) (OPTIONAL) The total cost of completing this case shall not under any circumstances exceed the sum of ______________Dollars ($________).

# HALT

HALT—An Organization of Americans For Legal Reform is a non-partisan public interest group of over 98,000 concerned citizens dedicated to reducing the cost and improving the quality of legal services in America. HALT is currently working at the state and national level to make our legal system less costly and more responsive to the needs of the average American.

HALT's program of reform includes:

- Producing educational materials to instruct citizens in the basic principles and procedures of our legal system. HALT's publications will make consumers sophisticated shoppers of legal services while increasing their self-reliance and ability to handle their own affairs.
- Simplifying the language of the law. HALT is seeking to ensure that all legislation and standard legal documents are written in clear and concise English. HALT is supporting several of the "plain language" bills now pending in state legislatures across the country.
- Protecting consumers of legal services through public participation and control in attorney grievance committees. Citizens must have a voice in protecting the public from professional misconduct.
- Reducing the cost and complexity of probate. HALT is introducing legislation in several states that will abolish attorneys' percentage fees for probate work and will require the state to provide instructional material for consumers who want to probate an estate themselves.

HALT is also working on divorce and real estate reform. It supports measures to reduce the incidence of unnecessary litigation, including the establishment of no-fault accident insurance.

HALT's reform program is an ambitious one, but great progress has already been made. Since its creation in 1977, HALT has made notable advances in the struggle for a better and more responsive legal system.

HALT was instrumental in passage of S.423—The Dispute Resolution Act, which provides for resolving disputes inexpensively at the community level without lawyers and formal courtroom procedures. Through its Judicial Integrity Project, HALT has supported investigation by prize-winning journalists into the unethical and incompetent behavior of judges at the federal level. HALT was the principal supporter of the Judicial Conduct and Disabilities Act of 1980, which will provide a means other than impeachment to discipline federal judges.

If you would like to join HALT or renew your membership, clip or copy the coupon below and mail it to HALT—An Organization of Americans For Legal Reform.

**HALT** 201 Massachusetts Ave., N.E., Suite 319
Washington, D.C. 20002

☐ YES! I want to help reform America's legal system *and* receive a FREE series of *Citizens Legal Manuals.* Here's my *tax-deductible* contribution for a one-year membership in HALT.

☐ $15 ☐ $25 ☐ $50 ☐ $100 ☐ $250 ☐ $500 ☐ $1000

Name ______________________________

Address ______________________________

City ______________ State ______________ Zip ________

(Make checks payable to HALT.)

SH